Bernardo de Galvez

Hero of the American Revolution

Eduardo Ortiz

SCHOLASTIC INC.

New York Toronto London Auckland Sydney
Mexico City New Delhi Hong Kong Buenos Aires

Illustrations
Tristan Elwell

Printed in the U.S.A.

ISBN 0-439-59769-2

5 6 7 8 9 10 23 12 11 10 09 08 07

Contents

Welcome to This Book

Did you ever need the help of friends to do something you couldn't do alone? Well, America had friends who helped it win freedom from Britain. And one of America's best friends was Bernardo de Galvez.

Bernardo was the governor of Louisiana. Back then, Louisiana belonged to Spain. Spain had not yet joined the war against Britain. But Spain wanted Bernardo to help the Americans.

So, Bernardo became a hero of the American Revolution. But how?

Target Words These words will help you understand the American cause that Bernardo de Galvez supported.

- **liberty:** freedom
  The American Patriots wanted liberty.
- **rebel:** someone who fights against those who are in charge
  The British thought that the Patriots were rebels.
- **revolution:** an uprising by the people to change their country's government
  Bernardo helped the Patriots win the American Revolution.

Reader Tips Here's how to get the most out of this book.

- **Map Reading** The map on page 7 shows you where the battles in this book took place. The smaller map shows what America looked like in the late 1700s.
- **Sequence of Events** This biography tells about events in the life of Bernardo de Galvez. Look for signal words like *first, next,* and *then* to find the order of events.

CHAPTER

1

A Secret Mission

The American Patriots are in trouble. Can Bernardo help?

The American **Patriots** were fighting the British. The war had spread to the Midwest. But the Americans were in trouble.

Their leader, George Rogers Clark, had heard that the British were planning an attack at the Ohio River. If the British won, they could attack the American colonies from the west. And they could also attack from the east by sea. Then the American colonies would be surrounded!

Clark asked leaders in Virginia for supplies, men, guns, and food to beat the British. But they had none to spare.

Clark had just one chance left, Bernardo de Galvez. Bernardo was the **governor** of Louisiana, which was then a **colony** of Spain.

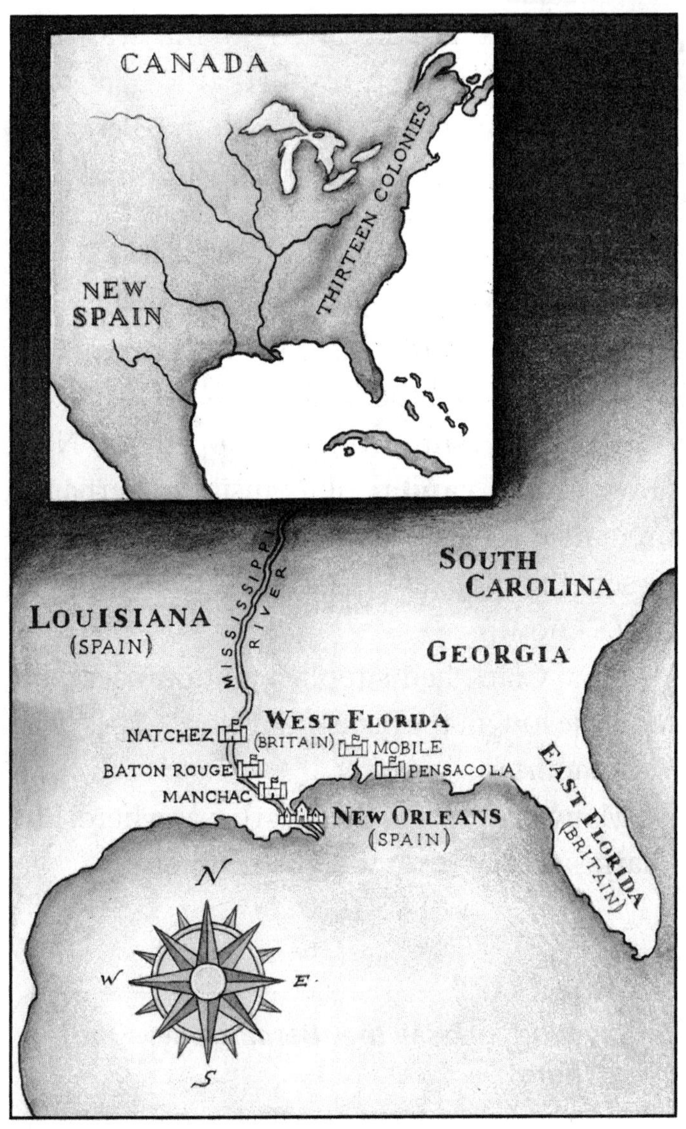

Bernardo was governor of Louisiana, which was a colony of Spain.

Spain was not involved in the war. But England was their enemy. Bernardo agreed to help Clark. But it had to be kept secret. Bernardo was taking a big risk. If the British found out, they would drag Spain into the war.

A Secret Plan

Finally, Bernardo came up with a plan. He was going to fool the British.

American ships often stopped in New Orleans, the **capital** of Louisiana. Bernardo pretended to **seize** and destroy them. Instead, he sent the supplies to Clark. The British would never know.

Now Clark had supplies, gunpowder, and food. He fought the British and won. Clark's win was important.

Many people said that Clark was a hero. But Clark said Bernardo was the real hero.

Heads Up!

Why did Clark say that Bernardo was the real hero?

About the American Revolution

Throughout the 1700s, Britain ruled the American colonies. The colonists had to pay taxes to Britain. The taxes got higher and higher.

Some colonists called for freedom from Britain. They wanted **liberty**. But Britain wanted to keep control of the colonies. A **revolution** broke out in 1775.

The colonists who fought the British called themselves Patriots. The Patriots wrote the **Declaration of Independence**. This stated that all men deserved to be free.

Spain had land in America too. And England was an old enemy. So Spain decided to help the Patriots. Bernardo de Galvez was governor of a Spanish colony in America. He helped a lot before Spain entered the war–and after.

In 1783, the British were defeated. The 13 American colonies would begin to form a new government. It would become the United States.

Without the help of Spain and Bernardo de Galvez, the Patriots might have lost the war. And things would be very different today!

CHAPTER

2

Born to Lead

Bernardo proves himself again and again.

Bernardo de Galvez was smart. He knew how to fight. He was a leader. And his men trusted him. The Patriots couldn't have asked for a better friend.

Bernardo was born in Spain in 1746. His family was very rich. Young Bernardo dreamed of becoming a great soldier. He joined the army when he was only 15 years old. He fought his first battle when he was just 16. Soon, he was leading troops.

Bernardo's father and uncles were soldiers, too. After the king, Bernardo's uncle was the most powerful man in Spain. This uncle took Bernardo to New Spain. New Spain was a Spanish colony in the Americas. The leader of New Spain gave Bernardo a risky job to do.

A Win for the Spanish

The Apaches, a Native American tribe, lived in New Spain. They did not like the Spanish settlers. The Spanish settlers had taken their land. So the Apaches fought back. The leader of New Spain asked Bernardo to protect the colony from Apache attacks.

Bernardo went after the Apaches. He led his soldiers on horseback. The journey was difficult. After a few days, the soldiers reached a river. They were tired and hungry. "Let us go back to our fort," they said. "We have food there."

"Sleep," Bernardo told them. "We will talk about it in the morning."

Morning came. The men got on their horses. They had decided to go home. But then Bernardo spoke. "Go home if you must," he said. "But I am loyal to the king. If I have to, I will go alone and fight to my death!"

Heads Up!

What do you think happened next? Would the men go home or fight?

Then Bernardo rode his horse across the river. His men saw how brave Bernardo was. They knew he would be killed if he went alone. "I will follow you!" one man yelled. "You are brave, Bernardo!" cried another.

Soon all the men rode their horses to Bernardo's side.

Suddenly, the Apaches attacked! Arrows flew. Some of Bernardo's men went down. Bernardo charged to the front of the line. The Apaches shot him with an arrow. Then they stabbed him with a spear. But still he fought.

After that battle, the Apaches stopped their attacks on the settlers. The settlers could stay.

The king rewarded Bernardo. He made him governor of Louisiana. Bernardo had no idea that his greatest battles were still to come.

Bernardo charged to the front of the line.

CHAPTER

3

Tricking the British

Bernardo thinks of many ways to help the Patriots.

As governor of Louisiana, Bernardo helped the Patriots many times. But he had to be careful. The British had spies in New Orleans.

Sometimes he pretended to seize and destroy American supplies. That's how he helped Clark. But that wasn't his only trick.

One day a ship full of guns and medicine landed at New Orleans. Bernardo claimed the goods were for his soldiers.

Bernardo went to look at the supplies. He acted shocked. "This medicine is old!" he said. "These guns are rusty! My men cannot use them."

A businessman pretended to buy the "damaged" goods. Then he secretly gave these

Bernardo went to look at the supplies.

supplies to the Patriots. The British guessed that it was all a trick. But they couldn't prove it. The businessman denied selling supplies to the Patriots. Bernardo just smiled and said, "I do not know anything about this."

New Flags for the Patriots

The Patriots were in trouble again. Farther up the Mississippi River, their soldiers needed supplies. But their boats could not travel.

A British colony, West Florida, was on the

right side of the river. When Patriot boats went by, the British would shoot at them.

Bernardo had a plan. He gave the Patriots Spanish flags. They put the flags on their boats. The British would not attack a Spanish ship.

Now the Patriots could send supplies to their soldiers. Bernardo had saved the day.

The British Question Bernardo

Spies told the British that Bernardo was helping the Patriots.

The British governor of West Florida asked Bernardo why. "Sir," he wrote, "you let American **rebels** put your flag on their boats. I am surprised."

Bernardo wrote back, "Sir, were those men really rebels? I am shocked!" Of course, he knew that the men were Patriots all along.

Bernardo knew that he could not keep playing games with the British. He worried that they might attack his colony. He got ready to defend his land. He made his army stronger. And he sent a spy to West Florida in 1778. The spy described the British forts to Bernardo.

Bernardo drew up a plan of attack. Then he put the plan away. But Bernardo knew he would need it soon.

And he did! In June 1779, Spain entered the war against Great Britain. Bernardo was ready. "At last!" he told his men. "Now we can fight the British in the open."

They would give the British a fight!

Heads Up!

The British used the word* rebel *in a negative way. What did the Americans call themselves instead?

CHAPTER

No Warning!

Three weeks, three forts.

Bernardo had learned that Spain and Britain were at war. But the British in West Florida hadn't heard the news yet. So, Bernardo decided to attack them before they found out.

The British had built some small forts on their side of the river. Bernardo's plan was to take these forts one by one.

The First Target

Bernardo attacked Fort Manchac first. It was about 90 miles north of New Orleans. Bernardo's army of 1,000 men walked the whole way. But they rested too, so they'd be ready to fight.

Bernardo's men attacked the fort at sunrise. Their gunfire woke the sleeping British! Bernardo and his men easily won the battle.

The Second Fort Falls

The next fort was at Baton Rouge. It would not be as easy to attack. The fort was new and strong. About 600 British soldiers protected it. But Bernardo had an idea.

One night Bernardo sent a small group of his soldiers to a hill outside the fort.

"Make as much noise as you can!" he told them.

The men chopped down trees. They built a wall of dirt. They worked all night long. And all night long the British shot cannonballs at this small group.

But in the morning, the British saw their mistake. They had been firing the wrong way!

Meanwhile, Bernardo's army had set up cannons on the other side of the fort. Boom! The Spanish cannons roared. They hit their

Heads Up!

Bernardo sent a small group of men to a hill outside the British fort. What did that small group of soldiers do next?

The Spanish cannons roared. The British soldiers screamed.

mark. Soon, the fort began to split apart. The British soldiers screamed. There was nothing they could do. Bernardo had won again!

Three for Three

A few days later, the Natchez fort fell without a fight. Only 60 British soldiers had been stationed there.

Bernardo had taken three forts in three weeks. Now Spain controlled the lower part of the Mississippi. American ships would be safe on the river.

But the British still controlled two strong forts. These forts were farther east. They were at Mobile and Pensacola. Bernardo wanted to win these two forts, too. But this time the British would be ready for him. Could he do it?

Heads Up!

Use the map on page 7 to trace the order of the battles. Which way did Bernardo and his men sail?

CHAPTER

5

Bernardo Battles On!

But will a storm stop him?

Bernardo decided that his next strike would be the fort at Mobile. It was on the Gulf of Mexico. Bernardo planned to attack by ship.

The mission had trouble from the start. Bad weather hit the ships. A strong wind blew several ships into sandbars. Two of those ships broke apart and sank. The men watched helplessly. Their guns, cannons, and other supplies dropped into the water. The men were ready to give up. But Bernardo remained strong. "Stay ready to fight!" he told his men.

Soon the storms stopped. At last, the ships made it to Mobile. And the fighting began. Bernardo gave the signal to fire. His soldiers hammered the fort with cannonballs. By sundown the battle was over. Bernardo and

Two of the ships broke apart and sank.

his men had won. More than 300 British troops **surrendered**.

Bernardo Calls for Backup

Bernardo's biggest fight was still ahead. Pensacola was about 60 miles east of Mobile. The British had many soldiers at Pensacola.

Bernardo needed help. So he went to the nearby island of Cuba. Cuba was also owned by Spain. There, he rounded up 64 ships. The ships carried 4,000 soldiers.

But bad luck struck again. His **fleet** sailed straight into a hurricane. The ships could not fight the winds and rain. They rocked back and forth. The men became sick.

"Turn back!" Bernardo ordered. He needed his men healthy and strong.

A few weeks later, Bernardo tried again. His men were rested. And the weather was perfect. His luck had turned. Or so it seemed.

Bernardo and his ships entered the bay leading to Pensacola. They had planned a surprise attack. But then the first ship hit a sandbar and got stuck! Now what?

"Yo solo!" Bernardo said. That means, "I alone!"

"Yo solo!"

The other ships refused to enter the bay. They did not want to get stuck, too. Bernardo's fleet had a problem. And the British were on their way.

Bernardo was on the warship *Galveztown.* He ordered his sailors to raise all the sails. "*Yo solo!*" he said. That means, "I alone!" The *Galveztown* raced toward the **mouth** of the bay. It came near the sandbar. Would the *Galveztown* make it through?

No one dared breathe. All eyes were on the *Galveztown*. Many soldiers doubted that Bernardo's ship could make it. But it did. The ship sailed smoothly through the bay.

The Spanish soldiers cheered. "He did it! General Galvez sailed into the bay!"

Bernardo climbed into a rowboat. He stayed at the mouth of the bay guiding the other ships. Cannonballs slammed into the water around him. But Bernardo stayed calm. He waited there until his last ship had made it past the sandbar.

A Long Battle

At Pensacola, both sides fought hard. Smoke filled the air. Cannonballs flew and exploded. Bernardo and his men fought bravely from sunrise to sunset, week after week.

The men were tired. And they were hungry. But Bernardo was able to keep up their spirits.

Heads Up!

If you were Bernardo, what would you have said to give your men courage?

On they fought. Finally, after six long weeks, a lucky shot decided the battle. A Spanish cannonball hit some barrels of gunpowder near the fort. The gunpowder went off. The blast rocked the British fort. Black smoke covered the sky. Then a white flag appeared. The fight was over. The Spanish army had taken the fort at Pensacola!

Five months later, another British army lost another big battle. It was at Yorktown, Virginia. That battle ended the Revolutionary War. The Patriots had won! General Washington said that Bernardo had helped them win. Bernardo was a hero!

Heads Up!

Bernardo and his men fought a long battle at Pensacola. Which event ended it?

CHAPTER

6

Last Days

Bernardo had a soft side, too.

Bernardo went back to Spain. He was treated as a hero. The king gave him a coat of arms. This was an honor. A coat of arms is a family's special sign. Bernardo's coat of arms had the words "*Yo Solo*" on it. It also had a picture of the *Galveztown*.

In 1785, Bernardo returned to America as governor of New Spain. Bernardo was now in charge of all Spain's colonies there. That area included what is now Louisiana and Mexico. His wife and two children went with him.

Bernardo and his family moved to Mexico City. Mexico City was a sad place when they got there. People were hungry. Many were very sick. Bernardo bought food for poor families. And he visited sick people.

One day Bernardo saw three criminals who were about to be hanged. People nearby them were crying. "Sir," one said, "Spare these men. They do not deserve to die!" Bernardo stepped up to the hangman. "Don't kill these men," he said. "Send them to prison instead." The crowd cheered their kind leader.

One day in 1786, Bernardo began to feel very hot. It turned out to be a fever. He was so sick he could not work. He could not even get out of his bed. He died soon after. He was only 39 years old. His third daughter was born eight days after his death.

Bernardo died a hero. He had helped the Patriots win their freedom. And he had helped the people of New Spain. He was a brave man and a great leader. He would not be forgotten!

Heads Up!

If you had to give a speech telling why Bernardo was a hero, what would you say?

EPILOGUE

We remember Bernardo today.

In 1784, two years before he died, the United States Congress thanked Bernardo for his help.

But that's not the only thanks he received.

Galveston, Texas, is named after him. And a U.S. postage stamp honored him in 1980.

Today, a statue of Bernardo stands in Washington, D.C. The words under the statue are a reminder of what he did. The words say, "Spain offered the blood of her soldiers for the cause of American independence."

Bernardo's memory lives on!

Glossary

capital *(noun)* the governing city (p. 8)

colony *(noun)* a territory that is controlled by another country (p. 6)

Declaration of Independence *(noun)* a document declaring the freedom of the 13 American colonies from British rule (p. 9)

fleet *(noun)* a group of war ships under one command (p. 24)

governor *(noun)* the leader of a colony, territory, or state (p. 6)

liberty *(noun)* freedom (p. 9)

mouth *(noun)* the part of a river where it empties into another body of water (p. 25)

Patriots *(noun)* American fighters who went to war against the British for freedom (p. 6)

rebel *(noun)* someone who fights against those in charge (p. 16)

revolution *(noun)* a change of government (p. 9)

seize *(verb)* to take by force (p. 8)

surrender *(verb)* to give up in defeat (p. 24)

Index